Yearbook

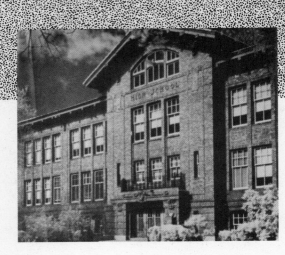

J.P. Richardson, Jr.
[Big Bopper]
Beaumont High School 1947
Beaumont, Tex.
Home Room President '45-'46;
President of Mixed Chorus '46-'47;
Football '46-'47; Tennis '46-'47.

Yearbook

by the Editors of **Memories** Magazine

A Dolphin Book

Doubleday

New York

London

Toronto

Sydney

Auckland

Acknowledgments:

This book could not have come together without the contribution of Seth Poppel and his fabulous collection of high school yearbooks, which MEMORIES magazine has long used and which was the source of more than half of the entries here.

Patty Greenbaum, Lisa Lewis, Anne Drake and Zazel Loven, all members of MEMORIES's staff, each worked tirelessly to augment Seth's collection. Miss Drake deserves special credit for dedication—and proofreading—above and beyond the call of duty. And if the book is any single individual's accomplishment, it is that of art director Andrea Gallo, who is responsible for the book's organization, look and feel.

Publisher Greg Coleman took the initiative to make it happen, literary agent Carol Mann found the exactly right publisher (with a little help from Diamandis Communications Inc. attorneys Catherine Flickinger and Yvette Miller), and Doubleday editor Paul Bresnick provided much-needed spiritual support and guidance.

And speaking of Diamandis Communications, no acknowledgment would be complete without heartfelt thanks to president and CEO Peter Diamandis, whose idea MEMORIES was in the first place and without whose support the magazine never would have happened.

Photos of Carol Burnett (p.13) and Ann-Margret (p.105) courtesy of Neal Peters

A Dolphin Book
Published by DOUBLEDAY
a division of Bantam Doubleday Dell Publishing Group, Inc.
666 Fifth Avenue, New York, New York 10103

DOLPHIN, DOUBLEDAY and the portrayal of two dolphins
are trademarks of Doubleday, a division of Bantam Doubleday Dell Publishing Group, Inc.

Library of Congress Cataloging-in-Publication Data

Yearbook / the editors of Memories.—1st ed.
p. cm.
    "A Dolphin book."
    A compilation of photographs from the high school yearbooks of celebrities.
    1. United States—Biography—Portraits. 2. Celebrities—United
States—Portraits. 3. Biography—20th century—Portraits.
4. School yearbooks—Humor. I. Memories.
CT220, Y43 1990
920.073—dc20   90-36473
                                                            CIP

Designed by Andrea L. Gallo, Class of '77
Cover Design by Whitney C. Cookman

Memories is a registered trademark of Diamandis Communications Inc.

ISBN 0-385-41625-3

Copyright © 1990 by Diamandis Communications Inc.

This book was born, as many things are, out of confusion. It was the spring of 1987 and everyone was running for President of the United States. Well, not everyone. A few of us were trying to invent a magazine about the recent past. MEMORIES, it was going to be called; that much we knew.

We also knew that we wanted it to be as different from the dry history courses of our school days as we could make it. We wanted it to be lively, irreverent, fun, witty, intelligent, thoughtful, relevant, entertaining—all the things we hope it turned out to be.

Most of our articles, we decided, would be "anniversary driven." That is, we would look at events of 20, 25, 30, 40 and 50 years ago with all the advantages of 20/20 hindsight, not only laying out what happened *then* but updating the story to *now*.

We also wanted to bring a perspective to contemporary events, like the Presidential campaign then looming so large on the political horizon. But how to make sense of a campaign that seemed to have as many candidates as voters? And one in which most of them seemed interchangeable. As Butch Cassidy put it to the Sundance Kid about the posse that kept stalking them, "Who *are* those guys?"

At a staff meeting, an editor spoke up. "I bet," the editor said, "you could get a better fix on who the candidates are and what they stand for by reading their high school yearbooks than by reading their position papers."

"Say that again!" I said.

The editor did.

And that's how our most popular feature started. That, too, though we didn't know it at the time, was how this volume was conceived.

Getting the yearbooks was more difficult than we had expected. First we had to track down where the candidates went to school. Some of the schools we contacted were obliging; others were not. Many wanted the candidates' permission, which meant more calls and letters. In the end, for our first issue, we came up with the yearbook photographs of 18 Presidential candidates, including the two eventual nominees, George Walker Bush (Phillips Academy, Andover, Mass., 1942) and Michael Dukakis (Brookline High School, Brookline, Mass., 1951).

Just as we hoped, the yearbook entries turned out to be wonderfully revealing, confirming a long-held conviction that high school is life and that who you are there is who you turn out to be. Thus, "Poppy" Bush was practically running Andover: president of the Society of Inquiry, chairman of the Student Deacons, president of the Greeks (funny, he didn't *look* Greek), captain of the soccer team and member of the editorial board of the school newspaper.

To no one's surprise, our yearbook feature was an immediate success. Most of the 1,000 letters we received about the new magazine asked for an encore. We were only too happy to oblige, and we've carried the feature ever since.

For the most part, the high-school-is-life rule has held true. Donald Trump was voted "Ladies' Man" of New York Military Academy's class of 1964. Robert Zimmerman (Bob Dylan) wanted "to join Little Richard" after graduating from Hibbing (Minn.) High School in 1959. Comedian Steve Martin was president of the Jason's Jesters Club at Garden Grove (Calif.) High School in 1963.

Writer Ray Bradbury was "headed for literary distinction" back in 1938 at Los Angeles High School, and Joyce Carol Oates had already discovered "the power of thought—the magic of words" at Williamsville (N.Y.) Central High School, 1956. Pat Sajak, Farragut High School, Chicago, 1964, wanted to become a radio announcer, and Oprah Winfrey was voted "most popular" in her class, 1971, at East High School in Nashville.

I could go on. But part of the pleasure of this book is making your own discoveries. And if you have half as much fun reading it as we have had putting it together, you're in for a treat.

—Carey Winfrey, Editor in Chief, *Memories* Magazine

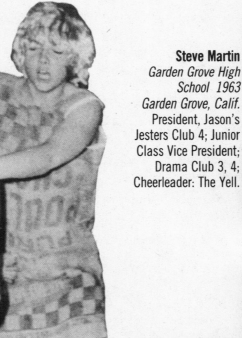

Steve

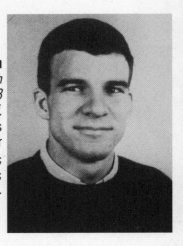

Steve Martin
*Garden Grove High
School 1963
Garden Grove, Calif.*
President, Jason's
Jesters Club 4; Junior
Class Vice President;
Drama Club 3, 4;
Cheerleader: The Yell.

Andrew G. Kaufman
*Great Neck North
Senior High School
1967, Great Neck, N.Y.*
"Andy."

Edward Murphy
Roosevelt Junior–Senior High School 1979
Roosevelt, N.Y.
"Murph"; Most Popular. Future plans: comedian. "In reality all men are sculptors, constantly chipping away the unwanted parts of their lives, trying to create their idea of a masterpiece."

Paul Rubenfeld
[Pee-wee Herman]
Sarasota High School 1970, Sarasota, Fla.
"Paul"; Pres., Theatre 70; National Thespian Society; Art Club; Advanced Mixed Chorus; Best Actor; Most Talented.

Paul

Class Clowns

Robin M. Williams
*Redwood High School
1969, Larkspur, Calif.*
Cross Country, Soccer.

Richard Gregory
*Charles Sumner High School
1952, St. Louis, Mo.*
Senior Class President.

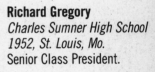

William J. Murray
*Loyola Academy 1968
Wilmette, Ill.*

James Leno
*Andover High School
1968, Andover, Mass.*
"Jay." Possible Future
Career: Retired
Millionaire.

Roseanne Barr
East High School 1970, Salt Lake City, Utah

Class ▼ Clowns

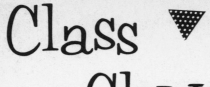

John Belushi
*Wheaton Central High School
1967, Wheaton, Ill.*
Class Council 2, 3; Forensics
4; Key Club 3, 4; Plays 3, 4;
Variety Show 2, 3, 4;
Thespians 3, 4; Secretary 4;
Choir 4; Football 1, 2, 3, 4,
Co-Captain 4; Wrestling 1;
Track 2, 3; Baseball 1;
Homecoming King 4.

John

Dick Smothers
*Redondo Union High School
1957, Redondo Beach, Calif.*
B Football; Track; Cross
Country; "R" Club; Sr. Play;
Jr. Play; Varsity Show 2, 3, 4;
Choir; Madrigal; Ivy Chain;
Head Cheerleader; Spanish
Club; Comm. of
Entertainment.

Thomas Smothers
*Redondo Union High School
1955, Redondo Beach, Calif.*
V. Football 4; Track 3, 4;
"R" Club; Varsity Show 4;
Key Club.

Art Carney
A.B. Davis High School 1935
Mount Vernon, N.Y.

Joe

George R. [Bob] Newhart
St. Ignatius College Prep
1947, Chicago, Ill.
Class Honors 2; Honors 1, 2;
Harlequins 1; Elocution
Finalist 3; Basketball 2. Bob
must have been a very
important person, because
people were always looking
for him. And every one of
them wore a white coat.

Joseph Charles John Piscopo
West Essex High School 1969
North Caldwell, N.J.
"A little fun to match each
day"; "All right!" agrees "Joe"
. . . likes Dean Martin, his
parties, surfing, acting, and the
bridge . . . Masquers-Pres, Law
Club, ABC, Drama, Soccer . . . a
career in either Law or the
Theater in the future.

11

Class Clowns

Gerald Stiller
Seward Park High School 1944
New York, N.Y.
"Boy! Has he got muscles!!"

Jack Cohen
[Rodney Dangerfield]
Richmond Hill High School
1939, Queens, N.Y.
Guard Duty, Intramural
Handball '38, Blue Cards,
Attendance Certificate,
P.S.A.L. Pins, He sleeps
by day.

Sidney Caesar
Yonkers High School 1937
Yonkers, N.Y.
Mechanical Drawing.

Dick Van Dyke
Danville High School 1944
Danville, Ill.
Junior Class President 3; Student
Council 2; Dramatic Club 1-4
(V. President 4); "Midnight" 2;
"Lease on Liberty" 3.

Leonard Hacker
[Buddy Hackett]
New Utrecht High School 1942
Brooklyn, N.Y.
There's laughs whenever he's
around.

Harvey Korman
Senn High School 1943
Chicago, Ill.
Players.

Carol Burnett
Hollywood High School 1951
Hollywood, Calif.

Lucille Ball
Jamestown High School
(9th grade) 1926
Jamestown, N.Y.
(center)

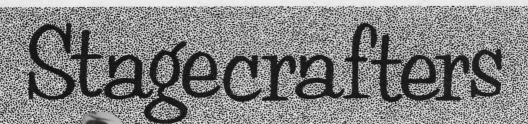

Meryl

Oklahoma!

Mary Louise Streep
Bernards High School 1967
Bernardsville, N.J.
"Meryl." Pretty blond . . . vivacious cheerleader . . . our homecoming queen . . . Many talents . . . Where the boys are. Gymnastics Club 1, 2, 3, 4; French Club, Sec. 1; J.V. Cheerleader 2; Varsity Cheerleader 3, 4; Chorus 1, 2, V.P. 3, Pres. 4; Class Treas. 1; Crimson 3; Bernardian Art Editor 4; Morning Announcer 3; Quill and Scroll, V.P. 4; Girls' State 3; Jr. Prom Comm. 3; Intramurals 1, 2, 3; Homecoming Queen, 4; Natl. Honor Soc. 4.

Warren Beaty [Beatty]
Washington-Lee High School 1955
Arlington, Va.
Varsity Football 2, 3, 4; Homeroom President 2; Junior Varsity Basketball 2; Officials Club 2; W-L Club 3, 4; Senior Class President 4; Best All-Around.

Richard Dreyfuss
Beverly Hills High School 1955
Beverly Hills, Calif.

Rick Dreyfuss states the play's theme.

Paul Newman
Shaker High School 1943
Shaker Heights, Ohio
Travel Club 2, 3; Booster 3, 4.

Clinton Eastwood
Oakland Technical High School
1949, Oakland, Calif.
Senior Day Committee, Senior
Banquet Committee.

Robert Redford
Van Nuys High School 1954
Van Nuys, Calif.

15

Stagecrafters

Jesse

Charlton Heston
New Trier High School 1941
Winnetka, Ill.
"Chuck"; Wilmette: Honor Groups
2, 3; Football 1, 2; "Whappin'
Wharf" 1; "Trelawney of the Wells"
3; "Death Takes a Holiday" 4; "The
American Way" 4; Inklings Staff 3;
Art League 1, 2, 3; Vice-President
3; Drama Club 1, 2, 3, 4;
Broadcasting Club 3, 4; Rifle
Club 1, 2.

Dustin Hoffman
Los Angeles High School 1955
Los Angeles, Calif.
"Dusty."

Jesse [Jessica] Lange
Cloquet High School 1967
Cloquet, Minn.
Pep Club 4; Book Club 4; Sno-Ball
Committee 4; White Pine 4; CHS
Reporter 4; Post Prom Committee
4; Senior Class Play 4; Detroit
Lakes High School 1, 2, 3. Artistic,
dramatic, and fun is she, a new
girl Cloquet was glad to see.

Harrison Ford
Maine Township High School 1960
Park Ridge/Des Plaines, Ill.
Social Science Club 4, President 4;
Boys' Club Representative 2, 3;
Model Railroad Club 1; Class
Council Representative 1, 2;
Variety Show 4; Gymnastics 1.

John [Jack] Nicholson
Manasquan High School 1954
Manasquan, N.J.
"Nick." Good natured . . .
enthusiastic writer of those English
compositions . . . his participation
added to our plays. Blue and Gray
1, 2, 4; Rules Club President 1, 2;
Football 1; Basketball Manager 2;
Study Club 3; Junior Play 3; Table
Tennis Club 3; Senior Play 4; Class
Vice-President 4.

Jack

Michelle Pfeiffer
Fountain Valley High School 1976
Fountain Valley, Calif.

CLASS CLOWNS

Stagecrafters

Don Johnson
*Wichita High School
South 1967
Wichita, Kan.
Senior Attendant;
portrayed Tony in West
Side Story.*

xxx
Don

Donald Jesse Knotts
*Morgantown High School
1942, Morgantown, W. Va*
Class President 2, 4;
Vice-President 3; Hi-Y 1,
2, 3, 4; Thespians 4;
Senior Follies 1; Hi-Y
Minstrel 1, 2, 3, 4; Us and
Co. Revue 1; Mardi Gras
4; Red and Blue Journal 4;
Student Council 1, 2, 3.

Cybill Shepherd
East High School 1968
Memphis, Tenn.
Charms strike the sight and merits win the soul. Cheerleader 1; Homeroom Officer 1; Pep Club 1, 2, 3, 4; French Club 3; Math Club 4; Science Club 4; East High Science Fair 1st Place; Homecoming Queen Candidate 4; Hall of Fame Most Attractive 4.

Philip Michael Thomas
San Bernardino High School 1967
San Bernardino, Calif.
Boys Choir, A Cappella Choir.

Priscilla Beaulieu [Presley]
H.H. Arnold High School 1963
Wiesbaden, West Germany
Best looking.

Alan L. Rachins
Brookline High School 1960
Brookline, Mass.
H.R. Chm. 1, 2; School Council 3, V. Pres. 4; Marshal 2, 3; Treas. N.E.S.G.A.; Var. Swimming 3, Capt. 4; Rep. to Mass. School Council Assoc. 3.

Mrs. P. I hope.

"IZZY"

Stage crafters

Isadore Demsky
[Kirk Douglas]
Wilbur H. Lynch Sr. High School
1934, Amsterdam, N.Y.
"Izzy"; Undecided; Alpha Beta
Gamma; Vice President Hi-Y; Cheer
Leader '33-'34; Usher. '31; Three
One-Act Play Contest '31-'32-'33;
Student Mixer '32-'33; "As the
Clock Strikes"; "The McMurray
Chin"; Student Councilor '31, '32;
Secretary and Treasurer of Junior
Class; Treasurer of Senior Class;
Junior Prize Speaking Winner;
Junior-Senior Frolic Committee;
Junior Ring Committee; Junior
Dance Committee; Senior Dance
Committee; Business Manager,
"Item"; Business Manager, Year
Book; Chairman, Class Day; Stage
Manager; Winner Edmund Dickson
Dramatic Prize; Delegate to Cornell
Press Conference; Second Recorder
Prize. "Not to know him argues
yourself unknown."

Roy Fitzgerald
[Rock Hudson]
New Trier High School 1943
Winnetka, Ill.
Winnetka: Swimming 1, 2; IM
Baseball 1, 2; Volleyball 1, 2, 3;
Glee Club 1, 2; Geography 1, 2;
Manual Arts, Los Angeles, Calif., 3;
Southern California.

Bernard Schwartz
[Tony Curtis]
Seward Park High School 1946
New York, N.Y.
"A good dancer, a good soldier and
a good sport."

20

Betty Bacal
[Lauren Bacall]
Julia Richman High School 1940
New York, N.Y.
News Columnist and Reporter;
Captain; Aide; Secretary; Inspector;
Property, Traffic, and Study
marshal; G.O. Representative.
Popular ways that win, May your
dreams of an actress overflow
the brim.

Mladen Sekulovich
[Karl Malden]
Emerson High School 1931
Gary, Ind.
Class President 4; Basketball '29,
'30, '31; Tennis Mgr. '29, '30, '31;
Opera '28, '29, '30; Board of Control;
Lake County Boys' Chorus '28, '29,
'30, '31; Spice and Variety '28, '29,
'30, '31; Concert Orchestra '28, '29;
Annual Staff; Senior Play. "The very
quietness of spirit"—*Merchant of
Venice.*

Anne Italiano
[Anne Bancroft]
Christopher Columbus High School
1948, Bronx, N.Y.
Gen. American Academy of
Dramatic Arts; Jr. Arista; Jr.
Leaders ; Dramatic Club; Eng.
Office. Proudly we'll say, "Anne's
been here."

"*Izzy*"

Richard Widmark
Princeton Township High School
1932, Princeton, Ill.
Class President 4, Vice President 3;
Football 2, 3, 4; French Club 4;
Science Club 4; Boys' Chorus 3;
National Athletic Scholarship Society
4; Hi-Y Club 2, 3, 4; Varsity Club 4;
Annual Staff 4; Newspaper Staff 4;
Class Play 3, 4; Senior Carnival;
Commencement Oration.

Stagecrafters

Tom

William Shatner
West Hill High School 1948
Montreal, Que. Canada
Football 2, 3, 4; Wrestling; Skiing
Club. Ambition: Actor. Nickname:
"Toughy."

Tom Selleck
U.S. Grant High School 1962
Van Nuys, Calif.

Larry Hagman
Weatherford High School 1949
Weatherford, Tex.
Los Hidalgos, Grass Burr Staff.

Bruce Walter Willis
Penns Grove High School 1973
Penns Grove, N.J.
Stu. Cncl. 1, 2, 3, Pres.; Perculator
Blues: Harps; Jr. Play, "D.C.5"; Sr.
Trip Judy in Kty.; Boogie Baby;
C.L.A.W.; Painting PMHS; MM at
Gino's; Fun at "Y"; Spec. Conc.; Jr.
Trip & food fights; "Magic Dick"
Cruisin; Blue's, Jeff, Murph,
George, Jay, David, John, Leighty,
Steve. Future: To become
deliriously happy or a professional
harp player.

Kim Basinger
Clarke Central High School 1971
Athens, Ga.
Y-Teens 1, 2; Pep Club 2, 3; SFCA
2; "A" Club 2, 3; DECA 3, 4;
Beauty Review 2, 3; Athens Junior
Miss; Homecoming Football
Sponsor; Jr. Varsity Football
Cheerleader 2; Varsity Football
Cheerleader 3.

James Maitland Stewart
Mercersburg Academy 1928
Mercersburg, Pa.
Indiana, Pa. "Jim," "Stew,"
"Elmer"; Main Hall; Marshall; Third
Football Team '24, '25, '26; Track
Squad '26; Karux Board '25, Art
Editor '26, '27, '28; Marshall
Orchestra '28; Choir '28; Glee Club
'28; Stony Batter Club '28; Class
Day Committee '28.

Venturing into a certain well-
known room in Main you are likely
to think you are interrupting the
prologue of a miniature Roxy, for
such is the disconcerting
impression created by the moving
strains of Jim's accordion and the
bellowing efforts of his
companions. Nor is music "Jim's"
only talent, for his skill in drawing
has long been the pride of the
Karux Board. In spite of Cicero's
best attempts to overcome him,
"Jim" is a good student and
invariably comes out on top.
Princeton

Henry J. Fonda
Central High School 1923
Omaha, Neb.
Hi-Y 3; Purple and White Week
1, 2. Henry has great ability in
art. He can detect a good picture
or a pretty girl with no trouble at all.

Marion Mitchell Morrison
[John Wayne]
Glendale Union High School 1925
Glendale, Calif.
"Duke"; University of Southern
California; Junior Class
Representative to Cabinet (3);
Vice-President Junior Class (3);
President Senior Class (4); Senior
Ring Committee (4); Explosion
Sport Writer (4); Honor Pin (2);
"Duley" (3); Southern California
Shakespearean Contest (3); Comites
(2); "G" Club (3), President (4);
Stage Crew (2), (3); Class B
Football (1), (2); Varsity Football
(3), (4).

« Officer 666 »

Tyrone E. Power
Purcell High School 1931
Cincinnati, Ohio
"Ty"; Dramatics '30, '31; Senior "B" Treasurer, '31; German Club '31; Class Basketball '29, '30. "Ty" came to Purcell from Dayton Prep, and in a short time became a favorite with students and teachers alike. "Ty" is a good student, but his acting makes him the logical successor of John Barrymore.

Shirley Beaty
[Shirley MacLaine]
Washington-Lee High School 1952
Arlington, Va.
"Shirl"; Cheerleader-Varsity 3, 4; Homeroom Sec. 2, 3, 4; Elos Play 4; Beta Tri-Y 3, 4; Variety Talent Club (Pres.) 4; French Club 3, 4. Laughing eyes . . . dancing feet . . . sparkling humor.

Shirl

James Dean
Fairmount High School 1949
Fairmount, Ind.
Basketball.

Dennis Lee Hopper
Helix High School 1954
La Mesa, Calif.
"Hopper"—our very talented actor. Favorite class is Drama. Won several speech contests. A.S.B. Play 2, 4; Choir 3, 4; Drama 2, 3, 4; Speech 2, 3, 4. "You'll Never Walk Alone." Most Likely to Succeed.

Sissy Spacek
Quitman High School 1968
Quitman, Tex.
Homecoming Queen.

Stagecrafters

Burton L. Reynolds
Palm Beach High School 1954
West Palm Beach, Fla.
"Buddy." Activities: Football, Track; Jr. and Sr. Superlative; Jr. Play; Key Club; Lettermen's Club; Student Council; Frond Staff; Basketball; B or Better Club. Life's Goal: To be as well liked as my father, and always have the friends I have now.

Samuel Pack Elliott
David Douglas High School 1962
Portland, Ore.
Transfer; S.B. Pres. 4; Exec. Council 4; B.L. Rep. 3; Choir 3; Vagabonds 3, 4; Ski Club 4; Regis 3, 4, Pres.; Metro Youth Advisory Council; Football 4; Track 2, 3, 4; Royal "D," 4; Voted Best Male Vocalist; Voted Best Personality.

Stagecrafters

Lindsay

Stacy

Stacy Keach
Van Nuys High School 1959
Van Nuys, Calif.

Lindsay Jean Ball
[Lindsay Wagner]
David Douglas High School 1966
Portland, Ore.
G.L. Class Rep. 3; Thespians 4;
Girls' Glee 4; Stage Door, Lead;
Stage Crew 4; Transfer 3.

Patti LuPone
Northport High School 1967
Northport, N.Y.
Voted: "most uninhibited," "most musical," "class clown," "most well-known person in school." Clubs: Band, Orchestra, Chorus, Student Government, Secretary.

Eugene M. Orowitz
[Michael Landon]
Edward C. Knight High School 1954, Collingswood, N.J.
1—"Ugy," "Emo"; 2—"Goofin' " off and listening to "Lindy's" adventures in wonderland; 3—Go to Istanbul with "Lindy," "Art," and "Al" in my "Rod"; 4—Track 2, 3, 4; Football 4; Class Vice-President 2; Varsity Club 2, 3, 4.

Kirstie L. Alley
Southeast High School 1969
Wichita, Kan.
B-Team Cheerleader 1; Pep Club 1, 2; "Spoon River Anthology" 3.

"UGY"

29

Stagecrafters

**Susan Abigail Tomalin
[Susan Sarandon]**
*Edison Township High School
1964, Edison, N.J.*
Academy of Sci. 3; Student Council
3, 4; Cheerleaders 4; G.A.A. 2, 3, 4;
Mes Amis 2, 3, 4; Mod. Dance Club
2, 3, 4; Class Rep. 1, 2, 4; Class
Officer 1, 2; Jr. & Sr. Class Plays.

John Lithgow
*Princeton High School 1963
Princeton, N.J.*
Versatile in the fine arts . . . "break
forth" grin . . . "Noah" . . .
Saturdays in the city . . . unruly
forelock . . . Activities: Student
Council President 4; School Play 3,
4; Tower Thespian President 3;
Member 4.

Jeff Goldblum
*West Mifflin North High School
1970, West Mifflin, Pa.*

Michael Kirk Douglas
The Choate School 1963
Wallingford, Conn.
1960-61: Football; Basketball; J.V. Track. 1961-62: J.V. Football; Wrestling; J.V. Track; Art Club; Auto Club. 1962-63: Varsity Football; Weight Training; Varsity Track; Chairman, Dance Committee; Art Club; President, Auto Club.

Dennis Quaid
Bellaire High School 1972
Houston, Tex.

Olympia G. Dukakis
Arlington High School 1949
Arlington, Mass.
Honor Roll, G.A.A., Ski Club, basketball, tennis, hockey. Our future gym teacher has chosen Sargent. "Limpey," who has personality galore, loves fencing. She also helped the memorable G.A.A. initiations to be such big successes.

Stagecrafters

Peter appeared as a private detective whose characterization brought forth peals of laughter and applause.

Peter Falk
Ossining High School 1945
Ossining, N.Y.
"Pete"; Class President 1, 4; Vice President 3; National Forensic League; Dramatics Club; Senior Class Play.

Patty Duke
Mace School (8th grade) 1960
New York, N.Y.
Even though Patty's famous, she has time for fun. She enjoys whatever she is doing and feels that that's all that counts. Though diminutive, her stature will undoubtedly be gigantic in the dramatic world.

Shelley Duvall
S.P. Waltrip Senior High School 1967, Houston, Tex.
Spanish Club '64-'65; Tri-Hi-Y '64.

Stephanie Powers
Hollywood High School 1960
Hollywood, Calif.

**Thomas C. Mapother IV
[Tom Cruise]**
*Glen Ridge High School
1980, Glen Ridge, N.J.*
Varsity Wrestling 11, 12
. . . Varsity Soccer 12 . . .
Varsity Club 12 . . . Key
Club 12.

Tom

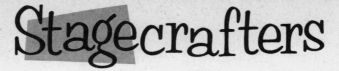

Stagecrafters

**Raquel Tejada
[Raquel Welch]**
*La Jolla Junior-Senior High School
1958, La Jolla, Calif.*
Cheerleader 11; Class Council
12, Veep 12; C.S.F. 11, 12;
Drama Club 10, 11, 12; Girl's
League Girl of the Week Chrm. 12;
Jazz Club 12; Mariners 12;
N.F.L. 10, 12; Rally
Co-Chrm. 12;
Sr. Play Chrm. 12;
Majors: Speech,
Drama; Career:
Actress;
Future: College.

Richard Chamberlain
*Beverly Hills High School 1952
Beverly Hills, Calif.*

Farrah Fawcett
*W.B. Ray High School 1965
Corpus Christi, Tex.*

Patrick Wayne Swayze
*Waltrip High School 1971
Houston, Tex.*
JV Football 1, 2; V. Football 3; FTA
3; Folk Singing 1, 2; Track 1, 2, 3;
Diving 3; Drama 1, 2, 3; Thespians
2, 3; West Side Story 2.

Natalie Wood
Van Nuys High School 1955
Van Nuys, Calif.

Ramon G. Estevez
[Martin Sheen]
Chaminade High School 1958
Dayton, Ohio
"Ray"; Variety Show 1, 2, 3, 4;
Intramurals 1, 2, 3, 4; Sodality 2, 3,
4; Speech 4; Dramatics 1, 2, 3, 4.

Ellen [Jaclyn] Smith
Mirabeau B. Lamar Senior High
School 1964, Houston, Tex.
(June) National Thespian Society,
Secretary '63; Kachina; Lamar-O-
Liers; Modern Dance Club;
Gym Leader.

Stagecrafters

**Norma Baker
[Marilyn Monroe]**
*University High School (10th gr.)
1942, West Los Angeles, Calif.*

Cheryl Stoppelmoor [Ladd]
*Huron Senior High School 1969
Huron, S.D.*
G.A.A., Spanish Club, Thespians (Sec.), Drama, Choir, Ensemble Work, Treble Clef, Varsity Cheerleader, Session Officer (V.P.), Senior Elections, Girls State (Alt.), Homecoming Attendant, Prom Comm., Tiger Day Float Comm., Miss Holiday.

Sally Kellerman
*Hollywood High School 1955
Hollywood, Calif.*

**Vera Jayne "Honey" Peers
[Jayne Mansfield]**
*Highland Park High School 1950
Dallas, Tex.*
Orchestra 1947-50; Hi-Lites 1947-50; Riding Club 1948; Orchestra Solo Contest 1947-49; Music Festival 1948, '49.

William [Willem] Dafoe
Appleton High School East 1973
Appleton, Wis.

Sean Penn
Santa Monica High School (11th grade) 1977
Santa Monica, Calif.

**Michael Douglas
[Michael Keaton]**
Montour High School 1969
McKeesrocks, Pa.

Daniel Travanti
Mary D. Bradford High School 1958, Kenosha, Wis.
Forensics 1, 2, 3; Football 1, 2, 3; A Cappella Choir 1, 2, 3; Honor Society 2, 3, Vice Pres. 2, Pres 3; K-Klub 2, 3, Sec. 2, Pres. 3; Class Vice Pres. Variety Show 3; SPY 3; Badger Boys State 2; Elks Leadership Contest, Second Place 3.

Danny

Stage crafters

Rodman Serling
*Binghamton Central High School
1943, Binghamton, N.Y.*
Football Intramural (2); Basketball
Intramural (2); Panorama Editor
(4); Drama "Excursion" (4); Debate
Club Vice President (3), Member
(4); Junior Red Cross Secretary (2),
President (3); G.O. (2, 3), President
(4); Scholarship (3); Honor Society
(4). After School: U.S. Army Air
Corps.

**Andrew Warhola
[Andy Warhol]**
*Schenley High School 1945
Pittsburgh, Pa.*
"Andy"; Home Room Sec. 205. As
genuine as a finger print.

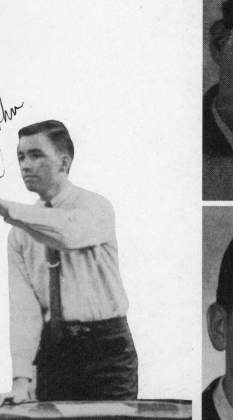

John Ritter
*Hollywood High School 1966
Hollywood, Calif.*
"Active in Student Body Government
affairs since the tenth grade, John
Ritter was elected President for the
Spring semester and proved that the
voters, as usual, knew what they
were doing."

Bob Englund
[Freddie Krueger]
Granada Hills High School 1965
Granada Hills, Calif.

Cassandra Peterson
[Elvira]
Palmer High School 1969
Colorado Springs, Col.
Office Monitor 2; Advanced A
Capella 2, 3; Girls Glee Club 1;
Interest: Art.

Cheryl Tiegs
Alhambra High School 1965
Alhambra, Calif.
College Prep; Songleader '64-'65;
Homecoming Princess '64; Junior
Council; La Hoalauna-Pres.,
V. Pres., Chap., Sec., Prexy Coun.

Jean Dorothy Seberg
Marshalltown Senior High School
1956, Marshalltown, Iowa
Y-Teens, 1, 2; Mixed Chorus 4,
Letter 4; Glee Club 2, 3; GAA 3, 4;
Pep Club 1, 2, 3, 4; Church League
2, 3; Band 1; Usher 4; G-Y 3, 4;
Cabinet 4; Pebbles Staff 1, 2;
Home Room Treasurer 1, Vice
President 4; Student Senate 1;
Masque and Dagger 3, 4, Letter 4;
Scholarship Society 3, 4; Plays 1,
2, 3; Play Contests 3, 4;
Co-President 1; G-Y Conference 3;
Music Groups 4; Oratorical
Contests 3; Girls' State Lt. Gov. 4.

Fred McFeely Rogers
Latrobe High School 1946
Latrobe, Pa.
College Preparatory—Mumbo
Jumbo 3; National Honor Society 3,
4; Quill and Scroll 3, 4; Oratorical
Finalist 4; Student Council
President 4; Latrobean Editor 4;
Extemp Winner 4.

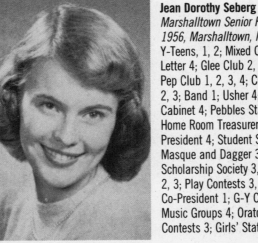

Kris Kristofferson
San Mateo High School 1954
San Mateo, Calif.
Vice President of Junior Class;
A.B.S. Vice-President; Varsity
Football and Track; Block SM
President; Vice-President of Saints
Hi-Y; Assemblyman to Y.M.C.A.
Youth and Government. Ambition—
Sports reporter.

Athletics

John

John Elway
Granada Hills High School
1979, Granada Hills, Calif.

[Sugar] Ray Leonard
Parkdale Senior High School
1975, Riverdale, Md.

Michael Jordan
Laney High School 1981, Wilmington, N.C.
Baseball 10, 11, 12; Basketball 10,
11, 12; Homeroom Rep. 10; Spanish
Club 11; FCA 10, 11, 12; Track 11;
New Hanover Hearing Board 12; Boys
State 11; Football 10; Pep Club 10.
To know basketball is one thing, but to
know you have the ability to be one of
the best is another. Mike Jordan wins
our hearts as he reaches for stardom.

Don Mattingly
Reitz Memorial High School 1979
Evansville, Ind.
Baseball.

Joe Montana
Ringgold High School 1974
Monongahela, Pa.
Academic—Baseball 1, 2, 3;
Basketball 1, 2, 3; Choir 3; Class
Vice-President 2, 3; Football Club
1, 2, 3; Football Team 1, 2, 3.

Joe Montana
pitches a fast one.

Nancy

Athletics

Joe

John McEnroe
Trinity School 1977
New York, N.Y.

Joseph Willie Namath
Beaver Falls Area High School 1961, Beaver Falls, Pa.
"Joe" . . . magician with a football . . . always ready to have fun . . . care-free. Audio-Visual Aides 11, 12; Knights o Safety 12; Pep 10; Varsity Club 12; Baseball 11, 12; Basketball, J.V. 10, 11, 12; Football 10, 11, 12; H.R. Secretary 10.

Walter Payton
Columbia High School 1971 Columbia, Miss.
Basketball 1, 2, 3, 4; Football 2, 3, 4; Hi-Y 1, 2, 3; Band 1, 2, 3; Choir 1, 2, 3; Science Club 2, 3; Track 2, 3; Baseball 2, 3; French Club 3, 4.

Patrick Ewing
Cambridge Rindge and Latin School
1981, Cambridge, Mass.
"Pat" . . . Basketball, Black Student
Union . . . College.

Nancy Lopez
Robert H. Goddard High School 1974
Roswell, N.M.
Nickname: Taco; Pet Peeve: Hard
teachers; Future Ambition:
Professional Golfer.

Jim McMahon
Roy High School 1977
Roy, Utah
Honors '75, '76, '77; Football '75, '76,
'77, Captain '77; Baseball '75, '76, '77;
Letterman's Club '75, '76, '77;
Basketball '76, '77; Black Knight
Award '76, '77; Baseball All-Area '76;
Football All-Area, All-Region, All-State
'76, First Team Quarterback '77;
All-Region Offensive M.V.P. '77;
4-A Division M.V.P. and Offensive
Back '77; Royal Guardsman '77.

Athletics

Sam Snead
Valley High School 1932
Hot Springs, Va.
"The world is blessed most by men who do things, and not by those who merely talk about it." Vice-President Sophomore Class, 1929- 30; President Glee Club 1931- 32; Member Orchestra 1931- 32.

Roger Staubach
Purcell High School 1960
Cincinnati, Ohio

Billie Moffitt
[Billie Jean King]
Long Beach Polytechnic High
School 1960
Long Beach, Calif.

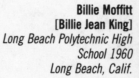

Vincent Edward [Bo] Jackson
McAdory High School 1982
McCalla, Ala.
Most Athletic, FFA, Teachers Aide, Var. Football, Jr. High Football, Vars. Baseball, Jr. High Baseball, Jr. High Wrestling, Track.

Wilton N. Chamberlain
Overbrook High School 1955
Philadelphia, Pa.
S.A., A.A., Basketball Captain,
Track, A.A. Representative,
School Improvement, Locker
Aide, Teacher's Aide.

Our favorite basketball player
kept the competitive teams
buoyed up for three years . . .
good food and music are
"George" with "The Dipper" . . .
hasn't time for talkative and
inquisitive people . . . dreams
of becoming an educated hobo.

Sandy Koufax
Lafayette High School 1953
Brooklyn, N.Y.
Varsity Basketball, Captain;
Varsity Baseball; Service
Squad; Cafeteria Squad. "To be
successful and make my family
proud of me." U.C.L.A.

Dave Winfield
Central High School 1969
St. Paul, Minn.

Terry Bolleo
[Hulk Hogan]
T.R. Robinson High School
1971, Tampa, Fla.

Athletics

Jack

James Nathaniel Brown
Manhasset High School 1953
Manhasset, N.Y.
"Jimmy"; Student Court 3; Chief
Justice 4; Football 1, 2, 3, 4, Letter
2, 3, 4; Basketball 1, 2, 3, 4, Letter
2, 3, 4; Lacrosse 1, 2, 3, Letter 1,
2, 3; Track 2, 3, 4, Letter 2, 3, 4;
Baseball 4.

Terry Bradshaw
Woodlawn High School 1966
Shreveport, La.
Safety Council 2; Football 2, 3, 4,
Letterman 3, 4; Track 2, 3, 4,
Letterman 2, 3, 4; ACCOLADE Court
3; Student Council Alt. 3; Red
Cross Rep. 3; French Club 4.

Jack William Nicklaus
Upper Arlington High School
1957, Columbus, Ohio
Basketball 1, 2, 3, 4; Hi-Y
3, 4; Golf 1, 2 (Captain),
3 (Co-Captain), 4; Student
Council 2; Varsity "A" 1, 2, 3, 4.

Mickey Mantle
Commerce High School 1949
Commerce, Okla.
They're great Pals, he and his baseball jacket. Football 3, 4; Basketball 1, 2, 3, 4; Tiger Chat 4; Bengal Tales; Baseball.

R.I.P.!

Athletics

John

Arnold Daniel Palmer
Latrobe High School 1947
Latrobe, Pa.
General . . . "Arnie" served on
Student Service . . . High Post
reporter . . . appeared in "Merchant
of Venice" . . . four year golfer . . .
Pennsylvania State Golf Champ.

Darryl Strawberry
Crenshaw High School 1980
Los Angeles, Calif.

Tom Seaver
Fresno High School 1962
Fresno, Calif.
Junior Varsity Baseball, Varsity
Baseball, B. Basketball, Varsity
Basketball.

Bill Russell
McClymonds High School 1952
Oakland, Calif.
Basketball.

Frank Gifford
Bakersfield High School 1948
Bakersfield, Calif.
Football.

John Joseph Havlicek
Bridgeport High School 1958
Bridgeport, Ohio
"Yunch," Freshman Class
President, Hi-Y President, Spanish
Club, Science Club, Football
Co-Captain, Basketball Co-
Captain, Baseball Team, Track
Team, Senior Class Vice-President,
Prom Committee , "Li'l Abner,"
Newspaper Staff, Scholarship
Team, Stagehand.

J. Edward [Jim] Rice
T.L. Hanna High School 1971
Anderson, S.C.

Wade Boggs
H.B. Plant High School 1976
Tampa, Fla.
Boys' State 3; Baseball 2, 3,
4; Football 2, 3, 4; Basketball
2; Letterman's Club 3, 4.

Gary Carter
Sunny Hills High School 1972
Fullerton, Calif.

Athletics

Don

Don Drysdale
Van Nuys High School 1954
Van Nuys, Calif.
Baseball.

Larry Joe Bird
Springs Valley High School
1974, French Lick, Ind.
Basketball.

Jack

Jack R. Robinson
*John Muir Technical High School
1937, Pasadena, Calif.*
Entered 3; Basketball 3, 4; Football
3, 4; Baseball 3, 4; Track 3, 4.

William Nuschler Clark Jr.
*Jesuit High School 1982
New Orleans, La.*
Big Brother—12, 11. French
Academy—11, 10. Intramural
Sports—12, 11, 10, 9, 8. Jayson—
12. NHS—12. Spirit Club—11.
Baseball 12, 11, 10, 9, 8.
Basketball 11, 10, 9, 8.

Mike Schmidt
*Fairview High School 1967
Dayton, Ohio*
Basketball; Baseball; Football;
Freshman Planning Comm.
Sgt.-at-Arms; Nobles Sgt.-at-Arms;
Prom Comm.; Spanish Club;
Varsity "F".

Ted Williams
*Herbert Hoover High School 1937
San Diego, Calif.*
Baseball.

Will

51

Athletics

Reginald Jackson
Cheltenham High School 1964
Wyncote, Pa.
Reggie . . . football Holden Award
winner and Co-Captain—Future
"All American" . . . basketball and
baseball star . . . hopes for
professional baseball . . . sports
cars . . . "screaming" '55 Chevy
. . . sovereign independence.

Johnny Bench
Binger High School 1965
Binger, Okla.
President 4; Basketball 1, 3, 4,
Caddo County All Star, State Tourn.
All Star, All State Team, Prep All
America; Baseball 1, 3, 4, All
State; Honor Roll 1, 2, 3, 4; Senior
Play; Annual Staff; Valedictorian.

Reggie

Gale E. Sayers
Central High School 1961
Omaha, Neb.
Basketball 1; Football 1, 2, 3, 4;
Inter-City Football 3, 4; Council
Bluffs Inter-City Football 3, 4;
All-State Football 4; 0-Club 1, 2, 3,
4; ROTC 1; Track 1, 2, 3, 4;
Wrestling 3.

Roger Maris
Shanley High School 1952
Fargo, N.D.
Football 3, 4; All-State 3, 4; All-
City 3, 4; Basketball 3, 4; Track 3,
4; Boys' State 3; Lettermen's Club
3, 4; Shack 3, 4.

Rick[e]y Henderson
Oakland Technical High School
1976, Oakland, Calif.
Baseball.

Ricky Henderson makes a base hit.

Versatile Gale Sayers starts
ascent over high hurdle.

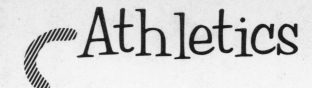

Athletics

Pete Rose
Western Hills High School 1959
Cincinnati, Ohio
Baseball.

Jack Clark
Gladstone High School 1973
Azusa, Calif.
Baseball.

Pete Rose acts fast
at the keystone.

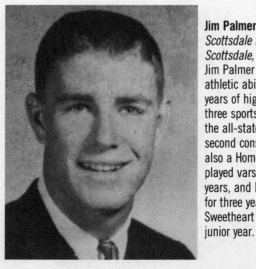

Jim Palmer
Scottsdale High School 1963
Scottsdale, Ariz.
Jim Palmer displayed unusual
athletic ability throughout his four
years of high school, lettering in
three sports. He was selected for
the all-state football team for his
second consecutive year, and was
also a Homecoming Attendant. Jim
played varsity football for two
years, and basketball and baseball
for three years. He was B.B.
Sweetheart Prom Attendant his
junior year.

Kirk Gibson
*Waterford-Kettering High School
1975, Drayton Plains, Mich.*

Kirk

Nolan Ryan
*Alvin High School 1965
Alvin, Tex.*
Baseball 2-4, All-District 3;
Basketball 3-4; Sophomore Vice-
President; Most Handsome 2, 4.

Bart Starr
*Sidney Lanier High School 1952
Montgomery, Ala.*
Football; Track; Basketball;
Baseball; "L" Club. Grand guy,
good sport, All-American, popular.

Bart

jerry

Dorrel

Kenneth M. Stabler
Foley High School 1964
Foley, Ala.
Art C.; Key C.; All State Football;
Most Athletic.

Dorrel [Whitey] Herzog
New Athens Community High
School 1959, New Athens, Ill.
"Relly"; "He likes girls even more
than basketball." Annual Staff 4;
Spotlight Staff 4; Boys' Quartet 3;
Lettermen's Club 2, 3, 4; Baseball
1, 2, 3, 4; Basketball 1, 3, 4, Capt.
4. Blasting out the ball for [an]
impressive average was R. Herzog
(.584). Prophecy: Relly is "Boy
Wonder of the Yankees."

Thurman Munson
John H. Lehman High School 1965
Canton, Ohio
Varsity Football 2, 3, 4; Varsity
Basketball 2, 3, 4; Frosh. Football
1; Frosh. Basketball 1; Baseball 1,
2, 3, 4.

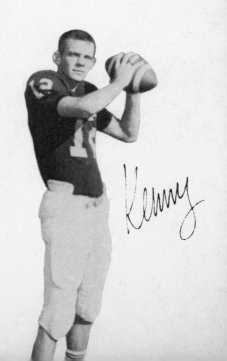

Kenny

56

Willie

Jerry Alan West
East Bank High School 1956
East Bank, W.Va.
Boys' State '55; Basketball '54,
'55, '56; Governor '56;
Shakespearean Literary Club '56.

Wilver Stargell
Encinal High School 1958
Alameda, Calif.
"Let me sing until I 'flat' myself to
death." J.V. Basketball; Var.
Basketball; J.V. Baseball; Var.
Baseball; Projection Club;
J.V. Football.

Alfred "Billy" Martin
Berkeley High School 1946
Berkeley, Calif.
Baseball.

OUT-
I SEZ HE'S
OUT.

SHADDAP YEZ
TRAMP HE
WAS SAFE!

NEVER A DULL MOMENT
WITH MARTIN AND DE ALBA
AROUND

JKD

**Chloe Wofford
[Toni Morrison]**
*Lorain High School 1949
Lorain, Ohio*
School Aide, Music, Senate Council, Clubs, Publications (Associate Editor), Dramatics, Class Officer (Treasurer), Senior Social Committee.

E.L. [Edgar] Doctorow
Bronx High School of Science 1948
Bronx, N.Y.
Intramurals, Dynamo, Yearbook

Erich Segal
Midwood High School 1954
Brooklyn, N.Y.
Senior Class President, Mayor of
City of Midwood, Junior Class
President, Varsity Soccer and
Track, Arista, Archon.

Truman G. Capote
Franklin High School 1943
New York, N.Y.
"Anxious for to shine
In the high esthetic line
As a man of culture rare."—Gilbert
Class Vice-President 4; Red and
Blue 4.

Robert Ludlum
The Cheshire Academy 1945
Cheshire, Conn.
"Lumpy," "Bob," "Johnny."
Football, Hockey, Tennis, Track,
Editor of *Academy Review*,
Chairman of War Fund, *Rolling
Stone*, Dramatic Club, Foote Club,
U.S.M.C. "I feel a flame within,
which does torment me."

Phyllis Anne Tyler
Broughton High School 1957
Raleigh, N.C.
"Artist" . . . "Seen with Meal?" . . .
"What's For Eats?" . . . Angier
Duke Scholar. Homeroom Officer 3,
4; Stage Crew 4; Latin Club 1, 2;
Little Theater 2, 3, 4, Treasurer 4;
Golden Masquers 3, 4; *Winged
Words* 3, 4; *Our Town* 2; *The
Fulfillment* 3.

Kurt Snarfield Vonnegut
Shortridge High School 1940
Indianapolis, Ind.
Student Council '38, '40;
President, Social Committee;
Drama League; Press Club;
Co-editor, *Tuesday's Echo,*
'40; *Annual* Liner Staff; "B"
band; R.O.T.C.; Junior Pin and
Ring Committee; Junior Party;
Co-chairman, winning act,
Junior Vaudeville '39;
Vaudeville '40; Round-Up
'38, '39; President, O.W.L.
Club; Chemist; Cornell.

Norman Mailer
Boys High School 1939
Brooklyn, N.Y.
Harvard University. Aeronautical
Engineer. Arista; Math Service;
Honorary President of Aviation
Club; Contributor, Editor of
Physical Scientist.

Bookworms

Ann O'Brien
[Anne Rice]
Richardson High School 1959
Richardson, Tex.
Fifth Place in State Rally for World
History 2; *Talon* Staff 4; GRA 4;
Dramatic Club 4; Press Club 4.

Joyce Carol Oates
Williamsville Central High School
1956, Williamsville, N.Y.
"Oatsie." Major: Science, Math,
French. Honor Roll 2, 3, 4; Chorus 4;
Billboard 3, Assoc. Editor 4; G.A.A. 2,
3, 4; Field Hockey 4; Basketball 3, 4;
Volleyball 2; Yearbook 4; Hi-Y 3, 4;
French Club 3, V. P. 4; Drama Club 4;
Intl. Club 4; News Editor 4; *Quill and
Scroll* 3, Pres. 4; Debate Club 4;
Literary Publication 4; "The power of
thought—the magic of words."

Gary [Garrison] Keillor
Anoka Senior High School 1960
Anoka, Minn.
Anokahi 3, 4; *Anokan* 4; Film
Operators 2, 3; Young Republicans
4. Gary wrote, typed, printed,
stapled and sold the *Varsity*, a
sports weekly. Gary confesses to
having discovered that journalism
has more problems than his
trigonometry textbook.

Ray Douglas Bradbury
Los Angeles High School 1938
Los Angeles, Calif.
L.A. Players Drama Club; Poetry
Club; Boys' Senior Glee. Likes to
write stories. Admired as a
Thespian. Headed for literary
distinction.

Bookworms

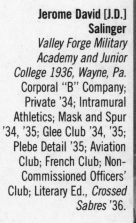

Steve

Margaret Mitchell
Washington Seminary 1918
Atlanta, Ga.

**Jerome David [J.D.]
Salinger**
*Valley Forge Military
Academy and Junior
College 1936, Wayne, Pa.*
Corporal "B" Company;
Private '34; Intramural
Athletics; Mask and Spur
'34, '35; Glee Club '34, '35;
Plebe Detail '35; Aviation
Club; French Club; Non-
Commissioned Officers'
Club; Literary Ed., *Crossed
Sabres* '36.

Eudora Alice Welty
Senior High School 1925
Jackson, Miss.
"Of talents and good things she owns such a store/You'd think where they come from there'd never be more." Secretary, Dramatic Club; Literary Editor, *Jackson Hi Life;* Art Staff, *Quadruplane* '25.

John Wilson Irving
Phillips Exeter Academy 1961
Exeter, N.H.
"Johnny," "Irv." College choice: undecided. Career choice: undecided. Student Council; Student Service Group (2); Red Key; J.V. Cross Country (2); Varsity Cross Country; J.V. Wrestling; Varsity Wrestling (3), Captain (1).

Robert Charles Benchley
Phillips Exeter Academy 1908
Exeter, N.H.
Worcester, Mass., "Bob," "Bench."
Entered Senior Year; Christian Fraternity; Deutscher Verein; Harvard Club; Bay State Club, Mandolin Club; Phillips Exeter Monthly Board; Alpha Nu.

Stephen King
Lisbon Falls High School 1965
Lisbon Falls, Me.
College Course. Honor Roll 1, 2;
Newspaper 2, 3, 4, Editor 3;
Senior Play 4.

God's Little Graduates

**Marion Gordon
[Pat] Robertson**
*The McCallie School 1946
Chattanooga, Tenn.*
Enrolled Sept. 1944; Private,
Company A '44-'45; Corporal,
Company C '45; Sergeant,
Company C '45; Varsity Football
'45; Varsity Boxing '44-'46; Varsity
Track '45; Y.M.C.A., '45-'46; Glee
Club '44-'46; Prefect '45-'46;
Virginia Club '44-'46.

William [Billy] Graham
*Sharon High School 1936
Charlotte, N.C.*
Baseball, first baseman. Ambition:
to become a preacher.

Jerry Laymon Falwell
*Brookville High School 1950
Lynchburg, Va.*
Valedictorian; Captain of Football
Team; Student Council; *Bee Line*
Editor-in-Chief. Favorite memory:
"Riding in Mr. Wright's car."

"His head is full of just what it
takes, Jerry should get all the
breaks."

Tamara La Valley [Bakker]
*International Falls High School
1960, International Falls, Minn.*
Choir 10, 11, 12. "Good things
come in small packages."

James Swaggart
*Ferriday High School 1952
Ferriday, La.*

Jim Bakker
*Muskegon High School 1959
Muskegon, Mich.*
Activities: Camera Club; *Campus
Keyhole* Editor; Masque; Director—
Varieties. Ambition: "To do the best
possible in everything I do."

Oral Roberts
*Atoka High School 1935
Atoka, Okla.*
Class President; Honor Student;
Editor of School Paper; Cheerleader
for Football Team; Basketball
Squad; Reporter for *Ada Evening
News*.

Candids

Everyone *loved*
Jesse Lange's hat!

James **Dean** plays
Frankenstein's monster.

Our M.V.P., **Vincent [Bo] Jackson**.

No one passes the ball like **Tommy Brokaw!**

Susan [Sarandon] Tomalin treads the boards.

Danny Travanti's star is on the rise!

Paul [Pee-wee Herman] Rubenfeld is leader of the pack.

Mike [Keaton] Douglas
is our star on the links.

GOLF

Jeff Goldblum asks,
"Waiter, is this a fly in my soup?"

Candids

Being cool is what
Ricky Henderson practices
all day long.

Jesse Lange is with
the hep crowd!

Hey, put on a happy face!
(Martin Sheen)

Michael Jordan
and his wheels.

Michael Landon and **Terry Bradshaw:** two seniors on the Hall of Fame highway.

The many faces of **Mary Louise Streep.**

Michael Douglas knows how to pass the time at Assembly.

Don Mattingly, sittin' pretty.

Candids

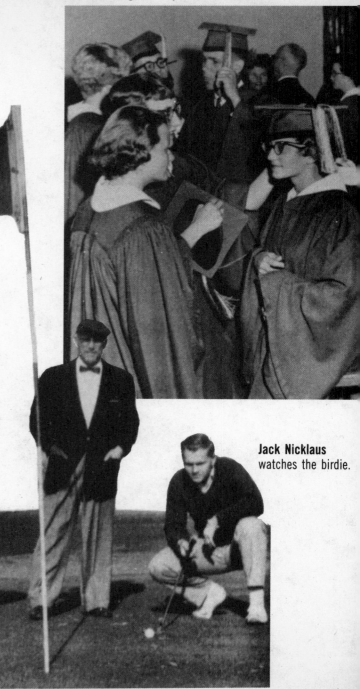

John McEnroe knows where his career will go if he doesn't practice.

No one beats **Reggie Jackson** on the field.

Jack Nicklaus watches the birdie.

Dan Travanti always looks sharp.

Michael Jackson has learned his "A-B-C"'s.

Bette Midler looks for a way to break into show business.

President **Bruce Willis** contemplates his post.

No one's a prettier cheerleader than **Cheryl Tiegs!**

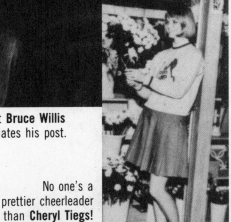

John Ritter, en route to the football opener in Las Vegas, sports his usual smile.

Liberace's never too far from the ivories.

Formals

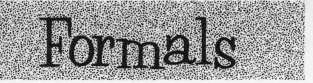

Bruce Willis has no heir apparent!

Joe Piscopo is our Master of Ceremonies.

Jesse Lange and date are all smiles!

Homecoming Queen **Sissy Spacek.**

Gary Carter can't dance, but he can still have a great time.

King-for-a-day **John Belushi** and his Queen.

Pretty **Cheryl Tiegs** takes a spin on the dance floor.

Bests

Paul Rubenfeld
Most Talented

Dennis Hopper
Most Likely to Succeed

Kenny Stabler
Most Athletic

Debbie Harry
Best Looking

John Lithgow
Most Creative

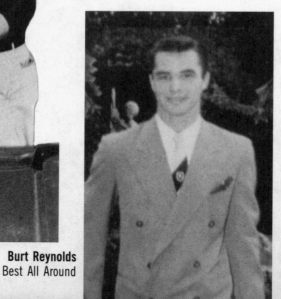

Burt Reynolds
Best All Around

John Belushi
Most Humorous

Shirley MacLaine
Most Talented

**Bruce
Willis**
Most
School
Spirit

Eddie Murphy
Most Popular

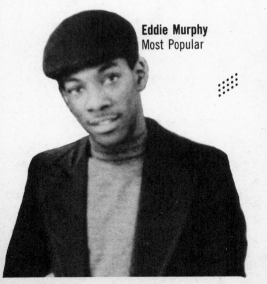

Cybill Shepherd
Most Attractive

Jack Nicholson
Best Actor

A.V. Squad

Directors

Francis Coppola
Great Neck High School 1956
Great Neck, N.Y.
"Francie." Attended New York
Military Academy 2, 3. Activities:
Band 4. Clubs: Junior Players 4.

Alan
Konigsberg
[Woody Allen]
Midwood High School 1953
Brooklyn, N.Y.

Shelton [Spike] Lee
John Dewey High School 1975
Brooklyn, N.Y.
"Smile, 'cause life is gonna be
what it is, there are brighter days
ahead."

Steve Spielberg
Arcadia High School 1964
Phoenix, Ariz.
Titan Band 12. "Spielberg seen as
talented actor."

Peter Bogdanovich
The Collegiate School 1957
New York, N.Y.
Dutchman 11, 12; Drama Club 9,
10; Glee Club 10, 11; Journal 9, 10,
11, 12; Yorkville Youth Council 10.
Earmark: Hairdo, precocious
wedding plans. Favorite Pastime:
Dinner for two at Nedicks.
Ambition: Actor. Probable
Occupation: Unemployed. "Bugs is
the anarchist of the Senior Class
when it comes to education."

Penny Marshall
Walton High School 1961
Bronx, N.Y.

Peter

Emote for me . . .

Directors

Brian De Palma
Friends' Central School 1958
Overbrook, Pa.
"Briar." Shameless . . . Flunks
physics . . . Soldier, statesman,
friend of the working girl (or any
other) . . . Just finished last year's
work . . . Have act, will produce . . .
Activities: Service Committee 9, 10,
11, 12 (President); Science Club 12
(President); "Wizard of Oz" 11;
"The Crucible" 12; Carnival 9, 10,
11, 12; Chess team 9, 10, 11, 12;
Model Congress 11; Soph Hop 10;
Junior Prom 11; Senior Prom 12;
Yearbook 12; Delaware Valley
Science Fair First Prize 10;
Delaware Science Fair Gold Medal
11; National Science Fair Second
Prize 11; Sports: J.V. Football 10,
11; Varsity Football 12; J.V. Tennis
10, 11; Varsity Tennis 12.

Melvin Kaminsky
[Mel Brooks]
Eastern District High School 1944
Brooklyn, N.Y.
Class Day Committee, Senior
Council, Dean's Assistant, Fencing
Team. Ambition: To be President of
the U.S.

Ron Howard
John Burroughs High School 1972
Burbank, Calif.

George Lucas
*Thomas Downey High School
1962, Modesto, Calif.*
History. Tennis Team 12.

Star Reporters

Tom

Tom Brokaw
Yankton High School 1958
Yankton, S.D.
Football 2-4; Track 2-4;
Homeroom Pres. 2-4; Pres.
Student Council 4; Mardi Gras
Cand. 2-3; Wokesape 2-4;
Annual 3; Arickara Nominee 4;
Boys' State 3; "Y" Club 4; Quill
& Scroll 4; Jr. Play; All-School
Play; NFL 4; Canteen Council 2.
Hobbies: records, dancing.

Walter Cronkite
*San Jacinto High School
1933, Houston, Tex.*
Booster Club; Spanish
Club; Literary Club; Tennis
Club; Editor-in-Chief,
Campus Cub '33;
Co-Sports Editor, El Oroso,
'33; President Journalism
Club '32; Vodvil '31;
Band '31, '32, '33.

Peter Jennings
*Trinity College School
1955, Port Hope, Ontario*
Dramatic Society 1955;
Cricket, First Team
Colours 1955; Rugby, First
Team Colours 1955,
Co-Capt. 1953.

Dan Rather
*John H. Reagan High
School 1959
Houston, Tex.*

Constance Yu-Hwa Chung
*Montgomery Blair High
School 1964
Silver Spring, Md.*
Student Government 4
(Member-at-large); Class
Officer 3 (V.P.); H.R.
Officer 2 (Pres), 3 (Sec'y);
Class Comm. 2, 3 (Ch.),
4; Athletic Comm. 2;
Awards Comm. 3.

Star ★ Reporters

Margaret Jane Pauley
Warren Central High School 1968
Indianapolis, Ind.
Hi-C 2; Warrenettes 2-4; Pep Club
2-4; Student Council 2-4; NFL 2-4;
Board 4; DAR Award 4; Fall Sports
Queen Court 2-3; Prom Court 3;
Girls' State 3, Governor; Speech
Team 2-4.

Edward James [Ted] Koppel
McBurney School 1956
New York, N.Y.
"Dumbo." M Club 2-4; Varsity
Soccer 2-4; All-City Soccer Team 4;
Varsity Tennis 2; Varsity Fencing 2;
Varsity Track 1-3; Glee Club 2-4;
Drama Club 4; Student Government
1; *McBurneian* 2-4; *Lamp and
Laurel*; Key Club Editor 4; Winner,
Book Mart Contest 4; Library Squad
1; Safety Squad 4.

Barbara Walters
Birch Wathen School 1947
New York, N.Y.
"The glory of a firm, capacious mind."

Linda [Ellerbee] Smith
*Mirabeau B. Lamar High School
1962, Houston, Tex.*
(June) National Thespian Society,
Reserve; Lancer Staff, Cartoonist,
'61, '62; Lancer Representative; City
Archery Squad; Mirabeau; Artisans;
La Cinquantaine; C.S.U.; Kachina;
Gym Leader.

Linda

Sam Donaldson
New Mexico Military Academy 1951
Roswell, N.M.
Sam received high marks and was
promoted to Cadet Sergeant.

Lila Diane Sawyer
Seneca High School 1963
Louisville, Ky.
"In youth and beauty, wisdom is but
rare." NHS 11, 12; "Veep" 12; Pep
Club 9, 10, 11, 12; Beta Club 10,
11, 12; J.C.L. 9, 10; Latin Club 9, 10;
German Club 12; J.V. Chldr. 9, 10;
Calendar Girl 9, 10, 12; Ex. Bd of Jr.
Class; F.T.A. 9, 10, 11, 12; Debate
Club 11, 12; "Arrow" Staff 10, 11,
12, Feat. Ed. 11, Ed-in-Chief 12; BB
Queen 10; Quill and Scroll 11, 12;
Youth Speaks 10, 11, 12; Cho. 9;
Madrigal 9; Jr. Play 11; Booster Club
10; Teen Club 9, 10; All Coun. Cho.
9; R.C. 9.

83

Talk Show Hosts

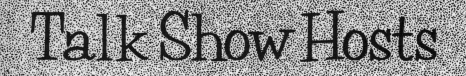

Arsenio Hall
*Warrensville Heights High School
1977, Warrensville, Ohio*

Johnny Carson
*Norfolk High School 1943
Norfolk, Neb.*
Features editor, *Milestone;*
best looking; most athletic.

Lawrence Zeiger [Larry King]
*Lafayette High School 1951
Brooklyn, N.Y.*
Manager, Basketball Team; Prefect;
Cafeteria; Locker Squads; Radio
Announcer; University of
Connecticut.

Billy Don Moyers
*Marshall High School 1952
Marshall, Tex.*
"Balfour Award" [highest academic
honor]; Student Council; Homeroom
Representative; Associate Editor,
Parrot; Band; Cheerleader.

Patrick Sajdak [Sajak]
Farragut High School 1964
Chicago, Ill.
Favorite subject: geometry. Favorite teacher: Mr. Bruska. Ambition: radio announcer. Organizations: Senior Cabinet, Senior Honor Society, National Honor Society, Scroll. Awards: Scroll Letter, Civic Award Letter.

Joan Sandra Molinsky [Joan Rivers]
Adelphi Academy 1950, Brooklyn, N.Y.
Joan was delegated co-chairman of the Cavalcade because of all her previous efforts in theatrical activities. She performed in the '47 and '49 school Cavalcades and was v.p. of the Dramatic Club in '49. Although her principal interests are acting and lindying, her record on the art staff of the *Adelphian* and *Oracle* speaks for itself. Joan's original cartoons added flavor and freshness to the school newspaper. Keep up that alert spirit and ready wit, Joan, and you are bound to succeed.

Gerald[o] Rivera
West Babylon High School 1961
West Babylon, N.Y.
Boys' Leaders Club 11, 12; *Eagle Echoes* 10, 11, 12; Spanish Club 9, 10, 11, 12; Football 9, 10, 11, 12; Basketball 9; Wrestling 11, 12; Track 9, 10, 11, 12.

David Michael Letterman
Broad Ripple High School 1965
Indianapolis, Ind.
Basketball Fr., Res. 2; Track Fr., Res. 2; Ripples 2; Musical 4; Hall Monitor 4; Band 1-2.

85

Dick Cavett
Lincoln High School 1954
Lincoln, Neb.
Arts and Sciences, Student Council president, State Student Council president, Mummers Play leads, Opera, Band, Aeolian Choir, Boys Glee, Mummers, L Club, Varsity gymnastics letter, Debate Gold Medal, Boys' State, Joy Night central committee, Sophomore Assembly, honor roll, Joy Night, National Honor Society.

Philip J. Donahue
Saint Edward High School 1953
Lakewood, Ohio
Band, Dramatics, Thespian Society, *The Edwardian.*

Oprah Winfrey
East High School 1971
Nashville, Tenn.
Thespians 2; Drama Club 3, Pres. 3; N.F.L. 3, 4, Sec. 3, Pres. 4; State Forensic Champion 3; Student Council 3, 4, Pres. 4; Honor Society 4; Miss East High Finalist 3; Most Popular 4.

David Garroway
University City High School 1931
University, Mo.
Student Council 2; PEP Staff 2, 3; Dramatic Club 3, 4; President 3; Vice-President 4; Aero Squadron 2, 3; Debating Team 3; Golf Team 3, 4; Opera 3, 4; Principal 4; Senior Play 4; Chemistry Club 3; Service Club 2, 3, 4.

Fannye Rose [Dinah] Shore
Hume-Fogg High School 1934
Nashville, Tenn.
Academic; Latin Club '32; Dramatic Club '32, '33, '34; Research Chairman; Music Club '33, '34, Secretary '34; Student Cooperative Organization '33; Winner Girls' Declamatory Contest '33; Leland Hume Debate '34; Secretary-Treasurer Athletic Association Spring '34; Best All-Around Girl.

Student Government

Dwight David Eisenhower
Abilene High School 1909, Abilene, Kan.
Baseball, Football, Athletic Association Officer.

John Fitzgerald Kennedy
Choate School 1935
Boston, Mass.
"Jack," "Ken."
Age: 17. Height: 5 ft. 11 in. Weight: 155 lbs. Number of years in school: 4. 1931-32: League Football, League Basketball, League Baseball. 1932-33: League Football, Second Basketball Squad, Blue Basketball Team, *Brief* Board. 1933-34: Junior Football Team, Second Basketball Squad, *Brief* Board. 1934-35: Business Manager of the *Brief,* Golf Squad, Harvard.

Class Presidents

Lyndon B. Johnson
Johnson City High School 1924
Johnson City, Tex.
Public Speaking, Debate, Baseball.

Richard Nixon
Whittier High School 1930
Whittier, Calif.
Fullerton High 1, 2; Oratorical Contest
3, 4; Scholarship 1-4; Latin Club 4;
Manager Student Body; C. & W. Staff 4.

Gerald R. Ford
Grand Rapids South High School 1931
Grands Rapids, Mich.

Class Presidents

"Dutch"

James Earl Carter
Plains High School 1941
Plains, Ga.

Ronald Reagan
Dixon High School, 1928
Dixon, Ill.
"Dutch."
Pres. N.S. Student Body 4; Pres. 2; Play 3, 4; Dram. Club 3, 4, Pres. 4; Fresh.-Soph. Drama Club 1, 2, Pres. 2; Football 3, 4; Annual Staff; Hi-Y 3, 4, Vice Pres. 4; Art. 1, 2; Lit. Contest 2; Track 2, 3.

George Walker Bush
Phillips Academy, 1942
Andover, Mass.
"Pop," "Poppy."
Secretary, Student Council (1 term); President, Society of Inquiry (1941-42); Chairman, Student Deacons (1941-42); President, the Greeks (1940-42); Captain, Soccer (1941); Society of Inquiry (1940-42); Editorial Board, *The Phillipian* (1938-39); Business Board, POT POURRI (1940-42); Varsity Soccer (1939-41); J.V. Baseball (1939); Varsity Baseball (1941-42); Treasurer, Student Council (1 term); President, Senior Class (1 term); Student Council (1941-42); Senior Prom Committee; Advisory Board; Captain, Baseball (1942); Student Deacon (1940-42); All-Club Soccer (1938); Deputy Housemaster; Varsity Basketball (1941-42); Varsity Baseball (1940); Johns Hopkins Prize (1938).

Mamie Doud [Eisenhower]
Wolcott School For Girls 1914
Denver, Colo.

Jacqueline Bouvier [Kennedy]
Miss Porter's School 1947
Farmington, Conn.
"Jackie."
Favorite Song: "Lime House Blues." Always saying: "Play a rhumba next." Most known for: Wit. Aversion: People who ask if her horse is still alive. Where found: Laughing with Tucky. Ambition: Not to be a housewife.

Claudia [Lady Bird] Taylor [Johnson]
Marshall High School 1928
Marshall, Tex.
May Fete Princess 1928; graduated third in class.

Thelma [Pat] Ryan [Nixon]
Excelsior Union High School 1929, Norwalk, Calif.
Student Body Secretary 1929; Debate Team; Junior Class Play; Senior Class Play; Filibuster Club 1928; Les Marionettes; Girls' League Cabinet 1926. Pseudonym: Buddy. Intention: To run a boarding house. Liability: Her two brothers. Occupation: Watching Tom. Talent: Watching Bill.

Betty Bloomer [Ford]
*Grand Rapids Central High
School 1936
Grand Rapids, Mich.*

Rosalynn Smith [Carter]
*Plains High School 1944
Plains, Ga.
(second from left)*

Nancy Davis [Reagan]
*Girls' Latin High School 1939
Chicago, Ill.*
Nancy's social perfection is a
constant source of
amazement. . . . She can talk,
and even better listen
intelligently, to anyone. . . .
The cast of "First Lady" has
straggled in for rehearsal. . . .
When the fatal night comes
Nancy knows not only her own
lines but everybody else's. . . .

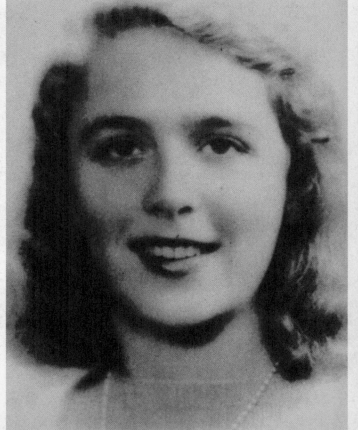

Barbara Pierce [Bush]
*Ashley Hall School 1943
Charleston, S.C.*

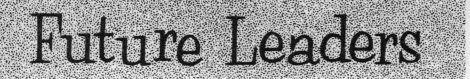

Future Leaders

James Danforth Quayle
Scottsdale High School (11th grade) 1963, Scottsdale, Ariz.

Danny Quayle demonstrates the proper grip.
Danny later shot an 80 and was the match's medalist.

Spiro Agnew
Forest Park High School 1937 Baltimore, Md.
"An ounce of wit is worth a pound of sorrow."

Gary W. Hartpence
Ottawa High School, Ottawa, Kan. 1954
Band 7-8-9-10-11; Kays 10-11-12, Treasurer 12; Dramatics Club 11-12; Boys' State 11; "O" Club 11-12; Football 8-9-10; Basketball 11; Track 10-12; Tennis 11-12; Record Managing Editor 12; Junior Play Cast; Class Vice-Pres 11.

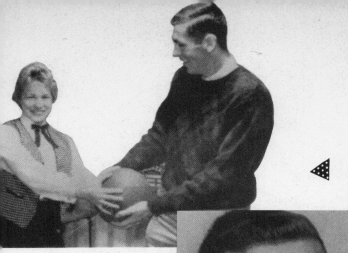

Neil A. Armstrong
Blume High School 1947
Wapakoneta, Ohio
"He thinks, he acts, 'tis done."
Band 2, 3, 4, Vice-President 4;
Orchestra 3; Glee Club 2; Student
Council 3, 4, Vice-President 4;
Retrospect Staff; Junior Hi-Y 2;
Senior Hi-Y 3, 4; Boosters Club 2,
3, 4; Junior Class Play; Home Room
President 3; Boys' State 3.

William Bradley
Crystal City High School 1961
Crystal City, Mo.
"Bill"; Basketball 1, 2, 3, 4;
Baseball 1, 2, 3, 4; Track 1, 2, 3,
4; M.A.S.C. President 4; "C" Club;
Student Council 1, 2, 3, 4,
President 4; Honor Society.

O. [Ollie] Laurence North
Ockawamick Central School 1961
Hudson, N.Y.
"I am not only witty in myself but
the cause that wit is in other
men." Track 2, 3, 4; Chorus 2, 3,
4; Chess Club 2, 3; Dramatics 4;
Student Council Alternate 4;
Service Squad 4; Science Club 4,
President.

John Glenn
New Concord High School 1939
New Concord, Ohio
"Herschel"; Hi-Y 1, 2, 3, 4; Cabinet
4; Hi-Y-G. R. Play 2, 3; Student
Council 1; Class Officer 2;
President 3; Newslite Staff 1, 2, 3,
4; Football 1, 2, 3, 4; Basketball 2,
3, 4; Tennis 1, 2, 3, 4; Varsity Club
4; Glee Club 3, 4; A Cappella 4;
Band 1, 2, 3, 4; Orchestra 1, 2, 3, 4.

Donald John Trump
*New York Military Academy,
1964, Cornwall-on-Hudson, N.Y.*

"D.T." Jamaica, N.Y. Entered 1959. Military Rank Achieved: Private, Company F, 1960; Corporal '61; Sergeant, Co. D., '62; Supply Sergeant, Co. E, '63; Captain, S-4, Senior Staff. Athletics: Varsity Baseball '62-'64; Varsity Football '62; Varsity Soccer '63; Intramural Basketball '62-'64. Bowling '62-'64; Softball '60, '61; Freshman Baseball '60, '61; JV Basketball '61; JV Football '60, '61; JV Wrestling '62; Wright Hall Bowling '60, '61. Activities: Columbus Day Parade, Commanding Officer, Composite Company '63; Cadet Council '63, '64; Honor Guard, Commanding Officer '63, '64; Fall Hop Committee '64; Varsity Letterman's Club '64; Driver Education Club '63, '64; Hobby and Model Club '60, '61. Academic Awards and Honors: Proficient Cadet '62, '63; Honor Cadet '60, '61, '63, '64. Awards, Medals, and Honors: Neatness and Order Medal '60, '61; Coach's Award, Baseball '64. Trophies: Intramural Softball '61; Basketball '64; Bowling '64; Freshman Football '60, '61. Letters: Varsity Football '62-'64; Varsity Football '62, '63; Varsity Soccer '63. Captain's Award, Baseball '64. Voted Popularity Poll's Class of 1964 Ladies' Man.

Hugh Hefner
Steinmetz High School 1944
Chicago, Ill.
Popular "Hef" cartoons, writes
songs and plays . . . goes for jive,
plaid shirts, corduroys . . . Student
Council, Star, Student Court, Green
Curtain Players, As We Like It,
Track, Choral Society.

Steven Jobs
Homestead High School 1972
Cupertino, Calif.

Lido Anthony Iacocca
Allentown High School 1942
Allentown, Pa.
"Lee."
Engineering and Science "When
you aim high at anything you are
sure to hit it."

National Honor Society 3, President
4; Orotan Debating Society 2, 3, 4;
Varsity A Club 4; Red Cross
Council 4; Latin Club 2, 3, 4;
Swimming Team, Manager 3, 4;
Junior, Senior and Interclass Play
Committee.

Lee is a raconteur extraordinary
and not only can he quip with the
best, but he can pun with the
worst. If knowledge really is power,
he is omnipotent. This, together
with the ability he has developed
in managing and directing school
affairs, will prove a great asset in
his career of engineering.

Michael Dammann Eisner
The Lawrenceville School 1960
Lawrenceville, N.J.
"Mike the Eyes," "But, sir!" Born
at Bedford Hills, New York, March
7, 1942. Inquirers Club '58-'60;
Hamill Football Coach '59-'60;
Hamill Basketball Coach '59-'60;
Periwig Club, acting '59-'60; *The
Lawrence* '56-'60; J.V. Basketball
'57-'59; J.V. Football '57-'58; J.V.
Tennis '56-'59; Thomas House
Treasurer '56-'57; *The Recorder*
'56-'57; Lower School Monitor
'59-'60; Done Most Extracurricular
Activities, Thomas House; Honors
'56-'57. Came to Lawrenceville
September, 1956. Houses: Thomas,
Hamill, Upper. Preparing for A.B. at
McGill University.

Class Officers

Ross Perot
Texas High School 1947
Texarkana, Tex.
Yearbook Business Manager

Roger Smith
Detroit University School 1942
Grosse Pointe, Mich.

Helen Gurley [Brown]
John H. Francis Polytechnic High
School 1939, Los Angeles, Calif.
Pres., Schol. Soc.; Pres., W.F.C.;
Pres., Amiticians; Cal. Schol. Fed.;
Ephebian; Athenian; Annual.

Sam Walton
David Henry Hickman High School
1936, Columbia, Mo.
Hats off to the President! Executive
Student President. . . . Presiding
over assemblies is just one of the
numerous duties of our president,
Sam Walton, affectionately known
by his many friends and
classmates as "Sammy." In
addition to his routine duties, the
president serves as our official
host at school, and as our
representative when away from it.
The highest office in our
democratic form of government
goes to one who earns it by his
leadership, service, and ability.
Sam Walton has gained this
distinction. Most Versatile Boy;
Latin '35, '36; Franklin Club '34,
'35, '36; Track '34; Torch '35, '36;
Library Club '35, '36; Forensic '34,
'35; Football '35, '36; Basketball
'36; Quill and Scroll '35, '36; Hi-Y
'35, '36; Magic Club '34; Class
Officer '36.

Malcolm Forbes
Lawrenceville School, 1937
Lawrenceville, N.J.
"B.C." "Male," "Sofa," *"That's my Pop!"*
Fountain Road, Englewood, N.J.
Born at New York, N.Y., August 19, 1919
Kennedy Rhinie Representative '35-'36; First
Prize in *Time* Magazine Current Events
Contest '35-'36, '36-'37; German Prize '36;
Essay Prize, Fourth Form, '36; Permanent
Member Cum Laude Society; Bibliophiles;
Vice President, Herodotus; Pipe and Quill
'36-'37; Publications Committee '36-'37;
Editor-in-Chief Olla Podrida '36-'37; Editor
Kennedy Eagle '35-'36; Lit '36-'37; Kennedy
House Debating Team '35-'36; Chairman,
Republican Committee, '36-'37; Flag
Speaker. Came to Lawrenceville September
1934. Preparing for Princeton. Last year an
unobtrusive rhinie entered the vaulted halls
of Kennedy and promptly won his first but
not last political campaign. B.C. endowed
with true political blood was elected rhinie
rep, and soon established himself as a
humorist, a gentleman, and a scholar.
Under his guidance the Kennedy Eagle was
nourished from a cheeping eaglet to a
powerful bronze ruler of the skies. A
permanent Cum Laude member this year
... B.C. has more than proven his
intellectual abilities. But it is as a generous
friend that we like him most. His unselfish
devotion to this edition of the Olla Podrida
is an excellent example of his industry and
capability. Even at that, B.C. is no grind.
His ability to understand "book larnin" is
as deep a mystery as why he persists in
wearing "Canal Boats." But for so talented
a youth, we forgive nonconformity and high
shoes. We have ample guarantee that B.C.
will follow in his father's footsteps. We do
not shout "Good Luck" for luck will have no
share in B.C.'s assured future success.

Glee Club

Brenda Webb
[Crystal Gayle]
Wabash High School 1970
Wabash, Ind.
National Honor Society; Homecoming
Court; Belles and Beaux Singing Group,
Sect., Vice-President; Booster Block;
Variety Show; Chorus.

Francis Sinatra
Demarest High School 1933
Hoboken, N.J.

Barbara [Barbra] Streisand
Erasmus Hall High School 1959
Brooklyn, N.Y.
Freshman Chorus 1, 2; Choral Club 2-4.

Lionel Richie
Joliet Township High School 1967
East Campus,
Joliet, Ill.
Lettermen's Club; Varsity Tennis.

Elvis Aron Presley
Humes High School 1953
Memphis, Tenn.
Major: Shop, History, English.
Activities: R.O.T.C., Biology
Club, English Club, History
Club, Speech Club.

Johnny

Glee Club

Bette Midler
Radford High School 1963
Honolulu, Hawaii
Senior Class President, Class Play 3.

Neil Sedaka
Abraham Lincoln High School 1956
Brooklyn, N.Y.
Supply Squad; Pres. Choral; Music Dir.
Class Night; Dance Band; Pianist for
Assembly.

Neil Diamond
Abraham Lincoln High School 1958
Brooklyn, N.Y.
Fencing Team; G.O. Councilman;
Choral; Sing; Class Nite.

Dolly Parton
Sevier County High School 1964
Sevierville, Tenn.
F.H.A. 1, 2, 3, 4; Sectional Officer 2, 4;
Homeroom Officer 1, 2, 3, 4; "Gay
Time" 3; Music Club 1.

Bette

John Mathis
George Washington High School 1954
San Francisco, Calif.
S.B. Treas.; Reg. Pres.; Ex. Coun.;
Swimming; Basketball; Music;
Basketball Team; Track Team; S.F.
State.

Connie Franconero
[Connie Francis]
Belleville High School 1955
Belleville, N.J.
Talented Connie hailed from Arts High
in her junior year . . . active Baker's
Dozen and Spotlight . . . has taken
social and modern dancing lessons
. . . likes singing, dancing, playing the
accordion, composing music, roller
skating, and being on TV programs
Saturdays . . . dislikes calories . . .
future includes studying script-writing
and television.

Johnny

103

Glee Club

Michael Jackson
*Montclair College Preparatory
(9th gr.) 1973
Van Nuys, Calif.*

Diana Ross
*Cass Technical High
School 1962
Detroit, Mich.
Graduate in Clothing
and Textiles Division.
Dwyer; Swim Team;
Y-Teens; Hall Guard;
Best Dressed 1962.*

Ann Margret Olson
[Ann-Margret]
New Trier High School 1959
Winnetka, Ill.

Walter Liberace
West Milwaukee High School 1937
West Milwaukee, Wis.
"Our Wally" has already made his claim,
With Paderewski, Gershwin and others of
fame. Mixer Orchestra, German Club,
Latin Club, Hi-Lights, Glee Club.

Judy Collins
East High School 1957
Denver, Colo.
All-City Choir; All-School Show; Christmas
Pageant; Concert Choir; Council Capers;
Drama Club; 1957 Club. "Singing folk
ballads while accompanying herself on
the guitar, Judy entertains the student
body in the Spotlight assembly."

Band

Roy Orbison
Wink High School 1954
Abilene, Texas
To lead a Western Band
Is his after school wish
And of course to marry
A beautiful dish.

Roy Orbison, center, and the Wink Westerners.

**Robert Zimmerman
[Bob Dylan]**
*Hibbing High School 1959
Hibbing, Minn.*
Latin Club 2; Social Studies Club 4.
Ambition: "To join Little Richard."

Bruce F. Springsteen
*Freehold Regional High School 1967
Freehold, N.J.*
"Bruce"; Freehold
Boro . . . College Prep.

Jim Morrison
*George Washington High School
1961, Alexandria, Va.*

Buddy Holley [Holly]
*Lubbock High School 1955
Lubbock, Tex.*
Musicians Guild '53; SOS '53;
Choralaires '53; Westernaires '54;
Wrangler '53; VIC No. 95 '54,
'55, V.P.

Band

Paul F. Simon
Forest Hills High School 1958
Forest Hills, N.Y.
Chorus; Law.

Ann Bullock
[Tina Turner]
Charles Sumner High School 1958
St. Louis, Mo.
Ambition: Entertainer.

Quincy Jones Jr.
Garfield High School 1950
Seattle, Wash.
Operetta; Pen Staff Artist; Chorus;
Orchestra; Band; Mid-Winter Concert;
Noon Program Committee; Student
Director of Swing Band; Funfest.

Arthur I. Garfunkel
Forest Hills High School 1958
Forest Hills, N.Y.
Music.

Janis Joplin
Thomas Jefferson High School
1960, Port Arthur, Tex.
Art Club '59, '60; FNA '58, '59; FTA
'57, '58; GRA '57, '58; Slide Rule
Club '58, '59; "B" Average Award
'57-'59.

Phil

Phil Spector
Fairfax High School 1957
Los Angeles, Calif.

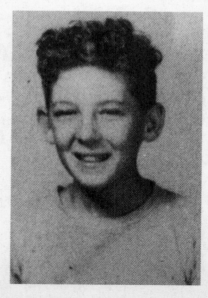

Jerry Lee Lewis
Ferriday Junior
High School (7th grade)
1950, Ferriday, La.

Deborah Ann Harry
Hawthorne High School 1963
Hawthorne, N.J.
College Prep; "Debbie." Ambition:
Undecided. Fencing Club, Secretary; Pins
and Needles Club, Secretary; Art Club;
1962 Graduation Usherette; Student
Council Regular; Junior Cabinet; Senior
Cabinet; *Ursidae* Staff, Art; Majorette;
Variety Show, 1 yr.; Dance Committees.
Best times: With Larry, lunch periods
with the girls, and at the basketball
games. Voted "Best Looking" in class.

Debbie
xxx

Edward Van Halen
Pasadena High School 1973
Pasadena, Calif.

Madonna Ciccone
Adams High School 1976
Rochester, Mich.
Thespian Society.

John Bongiovi
[Jon Bon Jovi]
Sayreville War Memorial High School
1980, Parlin, N.J.

Hugh Cregg
[Huey Lewis]
Lawrenceville School 1967
Lawrenceville, N.J.

Frank Zappa
*Joint Union High
School 1958
Lancaster, Calif.*

Did you go to high
school with someone
now famous? If so, we'd
very much like to hear
from you. Please write to
MEMORIES, Dept. Y, 1633
Broadway, New York,
N.Y. 10019. Please
include your phone
number if possible.